Welcome Home

Compiled by
Dan Zadra and Kristel Wills

Designed by
Steve Potter and Jenica Wilkie

COMPENDIUM™
PUBLISHING

live inspired.

ACKNOWLEDGEMENTS

These quotations were gathered lovingly but unscientifically over several years and/or were contributed by many friends or acquaintances. Some arrived—and survived in our files— on scraps of paper and may therefore be imperfectly worded or attributed. To the authors, contributors and original sources, our thanks, and where appropriate, our apologies.
—The Editors

WITH SPECIAL THANKS TO

Jason Aldrich, Gerry Baird, Jay Baird, Neil Beaton, Josie Bissett, Jan Catey, Doug Cruickshank, Jim Darragh, Jennifer & Matt Ellison, Rob Estes, Michael Flynn & Family, Shannan Frisbie, Jennifer Hurwitz, Heidi Jones, Cristal & Brad Olberg, Janet Potter & Family, Diane Roger, Jenica Wilkie, Clarie Yam & Erik Lee, Kobi, Heidi & Shale Yamada, Justi, Tote & Caden Yamada, Robert & Val Yamada, Kaz, Kristin, Kyle & Kendyl Yamada, Tai & Joy Yamada, Anne Zadra, August & Arline Zadra.

CREDITS

Compiled by Dan Zadra and Kristel Wills
Designed by Steve Potter and Jenica Wilkie

Printed in China

Celebrating the
Best Place on Earth

*It's not the size of the house,
but the love that dwells within.*

—Patricia Burlin Kennedy

"Home is the most popular, and will be the most enduring of all earthly establishments," wrote Channing Pollock. And we all know what he means.

It all begins with a dream. Somewhere in your mind's eye you begin to picture the perfect home, and that starts the magic. From there many hands, hearts and minds will combine to help make the dream a reality.

Someone helps you find your home. Someone helps you finance and insure it. Someone welcomes you to the neighborhood. And lots of friends and family drop by to take the tour and share in the housewarming.

Your home is more than just walls, doors and windows. It's your family foundation—the place where you'll build your dreams, plan your future, and create your memories.

Whether your home is large or small—cozy or grand—the same principle prevails. As Patricia Burlin Kennedy reminds us, "It's not the size of the house, but the love that dwells within."

Dan Zadra

Home is
a dream that
sometimes
comes true.

Anna Bohm

All that is worth cherishing begins
in the heart.

— *Suzanne Chapin*

Everyone has, I think, in some quiet
corner of their mind, an ideal home
waiting to become a reality.

— *Paige Rense*

There is no place more delightful
than home.

— *Cicero*

Home, in one form or another,
is the greatest object of life.

— *Josiah Gilbert Holland*

Your home is the one dream
you can actually walk into.

— *John Tuck*

I have learned that
even the smallest house
can make a home.

— *Henry David Thoreau*

There were no floors, no walls,
no ceilings, no windows and
the plumbing was nonexistent.
Of course, I fell in love.

— *David Utz*

I loved the house the way you would
any new house, because it is populated
by your future, the family of children,
friends and neighbors who will fill it with
noise or chaos and satisfying pleasures.

— *Jane Smiley*

My home is
where my favorite
memories are.

Pieter-Dirk Uys

A child on a farm sees a plane fly
overhead and dreams of a faraway place.
A traveler on a plane sees the farmhouse
below and dreams of home.

—Carl Burns

I remember, I remember
The house where I was born,
The little window where the sun
Came peeping in at morn.

—Thomas Hood

When you finally go back to your old hometown, you find it wasn't the old home you missed but your childhood.

— Sam Ewing

The companions of our childhood always possess a certain power over our minds which hardly any later friend can obtain.

— Mary Shelley

I have only to take up this or that to flood my soul with memories.

— Dorothee DeLuzy

We set off for school side by side, our feet in step, not touching but feeling as if we were joined at the shoulder, hip, ankle, not to mention heart.

— *Jamaica Kincaid*

We just wandered off along the path behind the school. We really weren't going anywhere, but when we felt like running, we just ran. The day was like that, and the things we did just happened.

— *Zilpha Keatley Snyder*

Home is the
one place in all
this world where
hearts are sure
of each other.

Frederick W. Robertson

Home is where one starts from.

— *Anna Jordan*

Home ought to be our clearinghouse,
the place from which we go forth
lessoned and disciplined, and ready for life.

— *Kathleen Norris*

I think the most significant work we
ever do, in the whole world, in our whole
life, is done within the four walls of our
own home.

— *Stephen R. Covey*

There are perhaps no days of our childhood we lived so fully as those we spent with our mothers and fathers in play.

— Dale Thomas

It ought to enter into the domestic policy of any parent to make her children feel that home is the happiest place in the world.

— Isabella Beeton

Never fear spoiling children by making them too happy. Happiness is the atmosphere in which all affections grow.

— Ann Eliza Bray

We didn't have much, but we
sure had plenty.

— Sherry Thomas

Any kid who has parents who are
interested in him and has a houseful
of books isn't poor.

— Sam Levenson

What a father or mother says to their
children is not heard by the world, but
it will be heard by posterity.

— Jean Paul Richter

My home is in
my mother's eyes.

George Nance

Many make a household but only one
make a home.

— James R. Lowell

Home to me is Mother;
home to me is love.

— Mary Loberg

A mother is a person who if she is not
there when you get home from school,
you wouldn't know how to get your
dinner and you wouldn't feel like eating
it anyway.

— Anonymous

Of all the gifts she gave us, please
The greatest of these
Were the memories.

— *Isabella Graham*

I cannot forget my mother. Though
not as sturdy as others, she was my
bridge. When I needed to get across,
she steadied herself long enough for me
to run across safely.

— *Renita Weems*

She made me a security blanket when
I was born. That faded green blanket
lasted just long enough for me to realize
that the security part came from her.

— *Alexander Cane*

Nowadays they say you need a special chip to put in the TV so kids can't watch this and that. In my home, in my day, we didn't need a chip. My mom was the chip.

— Ray Charles

A mother's happiness is like a beacon, lighting up the future but reflected also on the past in the guise of fond memories.

— Honoré de Balzac

It doesn't matter how old I get, whenever I see anything new or splendid, I want to call, "Mom, come and take a look."

— Helen Exley

Through thick
and thin, she
kept our house
open to hope.

John Katzer

Nobody knows of the work it takes
to keep the home together.
Nobody knows of the steps it takes.
Nobody knows but mother.

— *Anonymous*

What my mother did—not said—
gave me the courage to look ahead.

— *Ron Burton*

What did I learn at my mother's knee?
These four words: She believed in me.

— *Pat Baldwin*

Home is not where you live,
but where they understand you.

— *Christian Morgenstern*

A mother understands what a child
does not say.

— *Jewish Proverb*

A mother rejoices to see her young ones
leave the nest on their own, but she wants
to be sure they've packed a sweater.

— *Emily Broomfield*

We didn't always see eye to eye,
but we always saw heart to heart.

— Sam Levinson

Your love for your mother is something
that you never completely comprehend
until you are separated by the miles from
her warmth and her wonder.

— Collin McCarty

Children and mothers never truly part—
bound in the beating of each other's heart.

— Charlotte Gray

Home is where
a father's strength
surrounds and
protects his own…

Anna Vallance

Blessed is the man who hears many
gentle voices call him father!

— Lydia M. Child

All these years later, wherever I am,
I still hear Dad's laughter in the house,
still feel his love, still see his smile.

— Helen Marm

I associate the smell of new-cut grass with
my father, and sunny days, and happiness.

— Natasha Burns

Whenever I try to recall that long-ago
first day of school only one memory
shines through: my father held my hand.

— Marcelene Cox

My dear father! When I think of him,
it is always with his arms open wide to
love and comfort me.

— Isobel Field

He could mend almost anything—
a broken wagon or a broken heart.

— Dan Zadra

Whenever I did something as a little girl—learn to swim or act in a school play, for instance—he was fabulous. There would be this certain look in his eyes. It made me feel great.

— *Diane Keaton*

Secret learned in childhood and never forgotten: You can walk forever on a railroad track and never fall off—if you just reach across the track and hold your dad's hand.

— *Paul Gaither*

A father's lessons
are gifts that last
a lifetime.

Joan Aho Ryan

My father used to play with my brother
and me in the yard. Mother would come
out and say, "You're tearing up the grass."
Dad would reply, "We're not raising grass,
we're raising children."

— *Harmon Killebrew*

His heritage to his children wasn't words
or possessions, but an unspoken treasure,
the treasure of his example as a man and
a father.

— *Will Rogers, Jr.*

I talk and talk and talk, and I haven't taught
people in fifty years what my father taught
me in one week, simply by the way he lived.

— *Mario Cuomo*

It's not only children who grow. Parents do too. As much as we watch to see what our children do with their lives, they are watching us to see what we do with ours. I can't tell my children to reach for the sun. All I can do is reach for it myself.

— *Joyce Maynard*

My father didn't tell me how to live; he lived, and let me watch him do it.

— *Clarence Budington Kelland*

When I was a kid, my father told me every day, "You're the most wonderful child in the world, and you can do anything you want to."

— Jan Hutchins

You have been my light, my friend, my father—then and now—and more than that, my hero.

— Jiri Bedell

And though I know we are different, I am grateful for what I have of my father in me. It is my gift, my promise to myself and my children.

— Ken Barrett

Having a place to go—
is a home.
Having someone to love—
is a family.
Having both—is a blessing.

Donna Hedges

The family you come from isn't as
important as the family you're going
to have.

— *Ring Lardner*

My husband and I went to the hospital
as a couple, and came home as a family.

— *Theresa Little*

A baby will make love stronger, days
shorter, nights longer, bank rolls smaller,
homes happier, clothes shabbier, the past
forgotten and the future worth living for.

— *Anonymous*

What's the good of a home, if you are never in it?

— George and Weedon Grossmith

Children need your presence more than your presents.

— Rev. Jesse Jackson

The best things you can give children, next to good habits, are good memories.

— Sydney J. Harris

Happiness is family…home…evenings.

— *Unknown*

One of the luckiest things that can happen
to you in life is to have a happy childhood
and a loving home.

— *Agatha Christie*

Perhaps parents would enjoy their
children more if they stopped to realize
that the film of childhood can never be
run through for a second showing.

— *Evelyn Nown*

On Judgment Day
if God should say, Did you
clean your house today?
I will say, I did not.
I played with the children
and I forgot.

Sue Wall

A well-kept house is the sign of a misspent life.

— *Anonymous*

Mothers know that children are a house's natural enemy. They don't mean to be—they just can't help it.

— *Delia Ephron*

Cleaning your house while your kids are still growing is like shoveling the walk before it stops snowing.

— *Phyllis Diller*

A house is made to be lived in and not to be lived for.

— Ralph W. Sockman

Be careful. Housework can kill you if done right.

— Erma Bombeck

If your house is really a mess and a stranger comes to the door, greet him with, "Who could have done this? We have no enemies."

— Phyllis Diller

I hate housework! You make the beds,
you do the dishes—and six months later
you have to start all over again.

— *Joan Rivers*

Thank God for dirty dishes;
they have a tale to tell.
While other folk go hungry,
we're eating pretty well.
With home and health and happiness,
we shouldn't want to fuss;
For by this stack of evidence,
God's very good to us.

— *Unknown*

I will clean house
when Sears comes
out with a riding
vacuum cleaner.

Roseanne Barr

Nature abhors a vacuum. And so do I.

— Anne Gibbons

My idea of superwoman is someone
who scrubs her own floors.

— Bette Midler

I've got a self-cleaning oven—I have to
get up in the night to see if it's doing it.

— Victoria Wood

My second favorite household chore
is ironing. My first is hitting my head
on the top bunk bed until I faint.

— Erma Bombeck

I'm eighteen years behind in my ironing.
There's no use doing it now, it doesn't fit
anybody I know.

— Phyllis Diller

I buried a lot of my ironing in
the backyard.

— Phyllis Diller

My idea of housework is to sweep the room with a glance.

— Erma Bombeck

I would rather lie on a sofa than sweep beneath it.

— Shirley Conran

Have you ever taken anything out of the clothes basket because it had become, relatively, the cleaner thing?

— Katherine Whitehorn

Whenever Dad
was away from home
on a trip, Mom always
served us dessert first.

Annie Colello

Childhood smells of perfume
and brownies.

— *David Leavitt*

In the childhood memories of every
good cook, there's a large kitchen, a
warm stove, a simmering pot, and a mom.

— *Barbara Costikyan*

Whenever Mom baked pies, or cakes,
or even tuna casseroles, she would
always make miniature ones for us kids.
Your very own minature apple pie—
what a special treat.

— *Fred Dwyer*

Nothing rivals the healing powers
of a homemade fruit cobbler.

— *Anonymous*

When there is very little else left to
believe in, one can still believe in an
honest loaf of fragrant, home-baked bread.

— *Anna Thomas*

Love is like fresh bread. It has to be
re-made all the time, made new.

— *Ursula K. Le Guin*

A mother is a person who, seeing there are only four pieces of pie for five people, promptly announces she never did care for pie.

— Tenneva Jordan

Dad showed his love by taking a wing for himself and leaving the drumsticks for us.

— Don Ward

I never realized how much beauty lay around me in my parents' house: in the half cleared table, the tablecloth left awry, the knife beside the empty plate.

— Marcel Proust

No matter
where I take my guests,
it seems they like
my kitchen best.

Pennsylvania Dutch Saying

A good cook is like a sorceress who dispenses happiness.

— *Elsa Schiaparelli*

Laughter is always brightest where the food is the best.

— *Irish Proverb*

For those who love it, cooking is at once child's play and adult joy. And cooking done with care is an act of love.

— *Craig Claiborne*

I come from a family where gravy
is considered a beverage.

— Erma Bombeck

As a child, my family's menu consisted
of two choices: take it or leave it.

— Buddy Hackett

The most remarkable thing about my
mother is that for thirty years she served
the family nothing but leftovers. The
original meal has never been found.

— Alvin Trillen

Summer meant Mom's rhubarb pie,
ice cold watermelon and homemade
ice cream on the back porch.

— *Jon Fori*

Ice cream is the most evocative of
puddings. It brings back summer holidays
and the bicycle bell call of the hokey-
cokey man with his tricycle cart, and
rushing down the garden path with
Grandpa's big mug to have it filled for the
ice cream sodas which were invariably
constructed in tall sundae glasses.

— *Shona Crawford Poole*

Of course, the most indispensable ingredient of all good home cooking is love for those you are cooking for.

— *Sophia Loren*

Wherever one finds good food,
one also finds good companions.

— *Theognis*

Each of us eats about one thousand
meals each year. It is my belief that
we should make as many of these meals
as we can truly memorable.

— *Robert Carrier*

Sharing food with another human
being is an intimate act that should not
be indulged in lightly.

— *M. F. K. Fisher*

Cooking done with care is an act of love.

— *Craig Claiborne*

There is no sight on earth more appealing than the sight of a woman making dinner for someone she loves.

— *Thomas Wolfe*

A good cook is like a sorceress who dispenses happiness.

— *Elsa Schiaparelli*

Homemade food can look beautiful,
taste exquisite, smell wonderful, make
people feel good, bring them together,
inspire romantic feelings, help them to
share the best of life.

— *Rosamond Richardson*

After a perfect meal, we are more
susceptible to love than at any other time.

— *Hans Bazli*

That's something I've noticed about food:
whenever there's a crisis, if you can get
people to eat normally, things get better.

— *Madeleine L'Engle*

Won't you come
into my garden? I want
my roses to see you.

Richard B. Sheridan

My whole life is an adventure.
But you don't have to do something
racy and wild to have an adventure.
You can have one in your own backyard.

— *Gary Paulsen*

It's quite possible to leave your home for
a walk in the early morning air and return
a different person—beguiled, enchanted.

— *Mary Chase*

In my garden, after a rainfall, you can faintly,
yes, hear the breaking of new blooms.

— *Truman Capote*

People from a planet without flowers
would think we must be mad with joy the
whole time to have such things about us.

— *Iris Murdoch*

A garden isn't meant to be useful.
It's for joy.

— *Rumer Godden*

There can be no other occupation like
gardening in which, if you were to creep
behind someone at their work, you would
find them smiling.

— *Mirabel Osler*

Gardens and flowers have a way of bringing people together, drawing them from their homes.

—Clare Ansberry

So come, and slowly we will walk through green gardens and marvel at this strange and sweet world.

—Sylvia Plath

Throw open
the windows of
your home and let the
scenery of clouds and
sky enter your room!

Yosa Buson

There are moments on most days when
I feel a deep and sincere gratitude, when
I sit at the open window and there is a
blue sky or moving clouds.

— Kathe Kollwitz

Go to the window and look at the stars.

— Ralph Waldo Emerson

The only calendar I need is just outside my
window. With eyes to see and ears
to hear, nature keeps me posted.

— Alfred A. Montapert

Sit outside at midnight and close your eyes; feel the grass, the air, the space. Listen to birds for ten minutes at dawn. Memorize a flower.

— *Linda Hasselstrom*

I value my garden more for being full of blackbirds than of cherries, and very frankly give them fruit for their songs.

— *Joseph Addison*

When I was a kid, we had a birdhouse in the neighborhood, with a little sign above its door that read, "For rent for a song."

— *Dan Zadra*

Never miss an opportunity to sleep on
a screened porch.

— Unknown

I enjoy early mornings on the porch;
fresh corn; going barefoot; blueberries
and strawberries and raspberries; sleeping
without nightclothes or covers; the long
evenings and the texture of the low
western sun on fields that are still green.

— Donald M. Murray

It's difficult to think anything but
pleasant thoughts while eating a home-
grown tomato.

— Lewis Grizzard

Even if I knew
that tomorrow the
world would go to
pieces I would still
plant my apple trees.

Martin Luther King, Jr.

He that plants trees loves others
besides himself.

— *Thomas Fuller*

One generation plants the trees;
another gets the shade.

— *Chinese Proverb*

To own a bit of ground, to scratch it
with a hoe, to plant seeds and watch their
renewal of life—this is the commonest
delight of the race, the most satisfactory
thing a man can do.

— *Charles Dudley Warner*

A man's children and his garden both
reflect the amount of weeding done
during the growing season.

— *Unknown*

The wind rushing through the grass,
the thrush in the treetops, and children
tumbling in senseless mirth stir in us a
bright faith in life.

— *Donald Culross Peattie*

I lean and loaf at my ease observing
a spear of summer grass.

— *Walt Whitman*

Rest is not idleness, and to lie sometimes on the grass under the trees on a summer's day, listening to the murmur of water, or watching the clouds float across the sky is by no means a waste of time.

— Sir J. Lubbock

That's the best thing about walking, the journey itself. It doesn't matter much whether you get where you're going or not. You'll get there anyway. Every good hike brings you eventually back home.

— Edward Abbey

Where thou art,
that is Home.

Emily Dickinson

"Home" is any four walls that enclose
the right person.

— *Helen Rowland*

There is room in the smallest cottage
for a happy loving pair.

— *Friedrich von Schiller*

Come live with me, and be my love
And we will all the pleasures prove.

— *Christopher Marlowe*

They gave each other a smile with a future in it.

— *Ring Lardner*

Love does not consist of gazing at each other, but in looking together in the same direction.

— *Antoine de Saint-Exupéry*

Nobody has ever measured, even poets, how much a heart can hold.

— *Zelda Fitzgerald*

When you love someone, all your
saved-up wishes start coming out.

— Elizabeth Bowen

Being deeply loved by someone gives
you strength, while loving someone deeply
gives you courage.

— Lao-Tzu

Love has a way of making places sacred
and moments meaningful.

— Janet Hobson

Ah! Life grows lovely
where you are.

Mathilde Blind

The best thing to hold on to in life
is each other.

— *Audrey Hepburn*

"Where's home for you?" a stranger
asks a fellow traveler on a plane.
"Wherever she is," comes the reply, as
the man points to a picture of his wife.

— *Kathleen Norris*

A successful marriage requires
falling in love many times, always with
the same person.

— *Mignon McLaughlin*

Happiness is not perfected until
it is shared.

— *Jane Porter*

Anything, everything, little or big
becomes an adventure when the right
person shares it.

— *Kathleen Norris*

If you miss love, you miss life.

— *Leo Buscaglia*

Love doesn't make the world go 'round.
Love is what makes the ride worthwhile.

— *Franklin P. Jones*

And what do all the great words come
to in the end, but that—I love you—
I am at rest with you—I have come home.

— *Dorothy L. Sayers*

Think contentment the greatest wealth.

— *George Shelley*

There may be
snow on the roof,
but there's still a fire
in the fireplace.

George Burns

Grow old along with me!
The best is yet to be.

— *Robert Browning*

They made a happy couple and a happy
home. They were such close friends that
even when they were two worn-out old
people, they kept playing together like
half-crazy puppies.

— *Unknown*

In the end, nothing we do or say
in this lifetime will matter as much
as the way we have loved one another.

— *Daphne Rose Kingma*

In my heart are all the treasures that
I shall ever own; they are the memories
of all the old friends I have known.

— *Kimberly Knutsen*

If we celebrate the years behind us
they become stepping-stones of
strength and joy for the years ahead.

— *Unknown*

The two old men sat in silence
together, relishing memories of the past.
They are lifelong friends and need
no words to share their thoughts.
One quavers to the other, "May you
live a hundred years, and may I live
ninety-nine." The other nods his old
white head and gravely says,
"Let us go home together and
drink a cup of wine."

— Han Chi, "Old Friends"

A house needs a grandparent in it!

Louisa May Alcott

Just about the time a mother or father thinks their job is done, they become a grandmother and a grandfather.

— Edward S. Dreschnack

The family with an old person in it possesses a jewel.

— Chinese Proverb

Nobody can do for little children what grandparents do. Grandparents sort of sprinkle stardust over the lives of children.

— Alex Haley

The simplest toy in the home, one which even a little baby can operate, is called a grandparent.

— *Sam Levenson*

Grandparents are people with too much wisdom to let that stop them from making fools of themselves over their grandchildren.

— *Phil Moss*

If I had known how wonderful it would be to have grandchildren, I'd have had them first.

— *Lois Wyse*

When you teach your child, you teach
your child's child.

— Don Ward

You too, my mother, read me rhymes
For love of unforgotten times
And you may chance to hear once more
The little feet along the floor.

— Robert Louis Stevenson

Every heart
comes home for
the holidays.

Dan Zadra

Always leave a little room in your home
for holiday miracles.

— Thomas Wolfe

Celebrate the happiness that friends are
always giving. Make every day a holiday
and celebrate just living!

— Amanda Bradley

Fill your life with as many moments and
experiences of joy and passion as you
humanly can. Start with one experience
and build on it.

— Marcia Wieder

When we give what we can and give it with joy, we don't just renew the American tradition of giving, we also renew ourselves.

— Bill Clinton

You give but little when you give of your possessions. It is when you give of yourself that you truly give.

— Kahlil Gibran

The most vivid memories of holidays past are usually not of gifts given or received, but of the spirit of love, the special warmth of friendship, the cherished little habits of the home.

— Lois Rand

Every minute should be enjoyed
and savored.

—Earl Nightingale

My favorite time of the holidays is when
the children have torn open their loot and
delivered their verdicts and are looking to
you for something else…memories that
have nothing to do with things bought.

— Jamie Lee Curtis

Joy is not in things, it is in us.

— J. Holland

When you're with
a friend, your heart
has come home.

Emily Farrar

I trace my roots, not to my ancestors, but to my childhood friends.

— Carlos Menta

It is not that we belong to the past, but that the past belongs to us.

— Mary Autin

From quiet homes and first beginnings, out to the undiscovered ends, there's nothing worth the wear of winning, but laughter and the love of friends.

— Joseph Hilaire Belloc

Wherever you are it is your own friends
who make your world.

— William James

The greatest ornament of the house
is the friends who frequent it.

— Ralph Waldo Emerson

Friends feed each other's spirits and
dreams and hopes; they feed each other
with the things a soul needs to live.

— Glen Harrington-Hall

Oh, the fun of arriving at your friend's
house and feeling the spark that tells you
that you are going to have a good time.

— *Mark Hampton*

Who enters my house as a friend
will never be too early.

— *Flemish Proverb*

The best kind of friend is the kind you
can sit on a porch swing with, never say
a word, then walk away feeling like it was
the best conversation that you ever had.

— *Anonymous*

A good laugh is
sunshine in a house.

William Thackeray

Life is too short to be cranky.

— Beej Whitaker-Hawks

If you have only one smile in you, give it to the people you love. Don't be surly at home, then go out in the street and start grinning, "Good morning" at total strangers.

— Maya Angelou

The laughter in our home is its heart beating. Laughter leads us, kneads us and sometimes helps bleed us of torments and woes.

— Bob Talbert

Family jokes are the bond that keeps most families alive.

— Stella Benson

The highlight of my childhood was making my brother laugh so hard that food came out his nose.

— Garrison Keillor

It is bad to suppress laughter. It goes back down and spreads to your hips.

— Fred Allen

No matter where we are we need
those friends who trudge across from
their neighborhoods to ours.

— Stephen Peters

On the road between the homes
of friends, grass does not grow.

— Early American Proverb

Who puts the coffee on for two.
Who makes me laugh when I am blue.
No matter what I have to do—my friend,
there's always time for you.

— Unknown

The American Dream
is not to own your
own home, but to get
your kids out of it.

Dick Armey

The greatest gifts you can give your children are roots of responsibility and wings of independence.

— *Dennis Waitley*

You gave me wings, now let me fly.

— *Don Ward*

Where we love is home, home that our feet may leave, but not our hearts.

— *Oliver Wendell Holmes, Sr.*

A child enters your home and for the next twenty years makes so much noise you can hardly stand it. The child departs, leaving the house so silent you think you are going mad.

— *John Andrew Holmes*

The most important thing that parents can teach their children is how to get along without them.

— *Frank Clark*

We've had bad luck with our kids— they've all grown up.

— *Christopher Morley*

Our babies are not just "our children"—
they will be other people's husbands
and wives, parents of our grandchildren.

— *Mary S. Calderon*

Your children are always your babies,
even if they have gray hair.

— *Janet Leigh*

We make our friends;
we make our enemies;
but God sends our
next door neighbors.

G. K. Chesterton

A good neighbor will double the value
of your property.

— Dale Rumbaugh

As neighbors we began by simply chatting
over the hedge; then one of us would
squeeze through an opening in the
branches. Eventually we'd carved out
a small door in the leaves. Rather than
walking around front to the path, one of
us would ritually crouch and crawl through
to discuss the weather and our dreams.

— Kathryn Livingston

In summer, when doorstep life dominates,
the natural quality of the neighborhood
comes out.

— *Mary Kingsbury Simkhovitch*

The presence of my good neighbors
was a comfort; their daily comings and
goings served as a friendly counterpoint
to my own hectic schedule, and I knew
that whatever problem I might encounter
during the day (however large or small it
might be), I could count on them for help.

— *Kathryn Livingston*

Without a sense of caring, there can be
no sense of community.

— *Anthony J. D'Angelo*

When you look at a city, it's like
reading the hopes, aspirations and pride
of everyone who built it.

— *Jane Jacobs*

There can be hope only for a society
which acts as one big family, not as many
separate ones.

— *Anwar al-Sadat*

In love of home,
the love of country
has its rise.

Charles Dickens

The values of a nation begin in the homes
of its people.

— *Don Ward*

When the world seems large and
complex, we need to remember that
great world ideals all begin in some home
neighborhood.

— *Konrad Adenauer*

The strength of a nation derives from the
integrity of the home.

— *Confucius*

If everyone sweeps in front of their own door, the whole city will be clean.

— *Urban Proverb*

A feeling of home in the world comes through caring and being cared for.

— *Milton Mayeroff*

I want you to be concerned about your next door neighbor. Do you know your next door neighbor?

— *Mother Teresa*

One great, strong, unselfish soul in
every community could actually redeem
the world.

— *Elbert Hubbard*

One person can make a difference,
and every person must try.

— *John F. Kennedy*

The happiest people I know are people
who don't even think about being
happy. They just think about being good
neighbors, good people. And then
happiness sort of sneaks in the back
window while they are busy doing good.

— *Rabbi Harold Kushner*

The place
you are in
needs you today.

Katherine Logan

Citizenship is the chance to make
a difference to the place where
you belong.

— *Charles Handy*

I believe that one of the most
important things to learn in life is
that you can make a difference in
your community no matter who you
are or where you live.

— *Rosalynn Carter*

To make a difference is not a matter
of accident, a matter of casual occurrence
of the tides. People choose to make
a difference.

— *Maya Angelou*

Start right where you are, in your
own backyard. Distant fields always
look greener, but opportunity lies right
where you are. Take advantage of every
opportunity of service.

— *Robert Collier*

I am of the opinion that my life belongs
to the community, and as long as I live it is
my privilege to do for it whatever I can.

— *George Bernard Shaw*

I look forward to an America which will
not be afraid of grace and beauty, which
will protect the beauty of our natural
environment, which will preserve the great
old American houses and squares and
parks of our national past and which will
build handsome and balanced cities for
our future.

— *John F. Kennedy*

I just love this house.
I wanted it for so long.
Now I have something that's
made the waiting worth it.
This is my blood, sweat,
and tears!

Patsy Cline

Home remains the most popular and
the most enduring of all earthly dreams
and establishments.

— *Channing Pollock*

If I were asked to name the chief benefit
of the house, I should say: the house
protects the dreamer, the house allows
one to continue dreaming in peace.

— *Gaston Bachelard*

Ask yourself, "How long am I going to
work to make my dreams come true?"
I suggest you answer, "As long as it takes."

— *Jim Rohn*

Dreams come a size too big so that
we can grow into them.

— *Josie Bissett*

I could visualize my dream home in my
mind's eye long before I had actually
found it—and way before I believed I was
worthy of owning it.

— *Cat Lane*

Sometimes you have to believe it before
you can see it.

— *Denis Waitley*

Happy are those who dream dreams and are ready to do whatever it takes to make them come true.

— *Leon J. Suenens*

Dreams are the picture-making power of your imagination. They are the stuff of which life, hope, love, fun, and accomplishment are made. All great things are born there. Respect and nurture your dreams—believe in them—and bring them to the sunshine and the light.

— *Dan Zadra*

If we want something very badly, we can achieve it. It may take patience, very hard work, a real struggle, and a long time; but it can be for us.

— *Margo Jones*

Where are we
really going?
Always home!

Novalis

A man travels the world over in search of
what he needs and returns home to find it.

— George Moore

Home is a place you grow up wanting to
leave, and grow old wanting to get back to.

— John Ed Pearce

I have come back again to where
I belong; not an enchanted place,
but the walls are strong.

— Dorothy H. Rath

True belonging is born of relationships
not only to one another but to a place
of shared responsibilities and benefits.
We love not so much what we have
acquired as what we have made and
whom we have made it with.

— Robert Finch

When you look at your life, the greatest
happinesses are family happinesses.

— Dr. Joyce Brothers

Other things may change us, but we start
and end with family.

— Anthony Brandt

Home is the place there's no place like.

— *Charles Schulz*

Where we love is home, home that our
feet may leave, but not our hearts.

— *Oliver Wendell Holmes*

Eden is that old-fashioned house
we dwell in every day
Without suspecting our abode,
until we drive away.

— *Emily Dickinson*

Come, let us
warm both our hands
before the fire of life.

Walter Landor

I am beginning to learn that it is the sweet, simple things of life which are the real ones after all.

— Laura Ingalls Wilder

There is no place more delightful than one's own fireplace.

— Cicero

You are a king or queen by your own fireside, as much as any monarch on the throne.

— Miguel De Cervantes

Home interprets heaven. Home is heaven
for beginners.

— Charles H. Parkhurst

To be alive, to be able to see, to walk,
to have my house, music, paintings—
it's all a miracle. I have adopted the
technique of living life from miracle
to miracle.

— Arthur Rubinstein

In the end the simplest questions are the
most profound. Where were you born?
Where is your home? Where are you
going? What are you doing?

— Richard Bach

The ordinary acts we practice every day
at home are of more importance to the
soul than their simplicity might suggest.

— *Thomas Moore*

We need not power or splendor,
Wide hall or lordly dome;
The good, the true, the tender,
These form the wealth of home.

— *Sarah J. Hale*

There are two things to aim at in life:
first, to get what you want; and after that,
to enjoy it. Only the wisest achieve the
second.

— *Logan Pearsall Smith*

Where your pleasure is, there is your treasure; where your treasure, there your heart; where your heart, there your happiness.

— St. Augustine

I have never been a millionaire. But I have enjoyed a great meal, a crackling fire, a glorious sunset, a walk with a friend, a hug from a child, and a kiss behind the ear. There are plenty of life's tiny delights for all of us.

— Jack Anthony

May you have warm
words on a cold evening,
a full moon on a dark night,
and the road downhill all
the way to your door.

Irish Blessing

Other "Gift of Inspiration" books available:

Be Happy
**Remember to live, love,
laugh and learn**

Be the Difference

Because of You
Celebrating the Difference You Make

Brilliance
**Uncommon voices from
uncommon women**

Commitment to Excellence
Celebrating the Very Best

Diversity
Celebrating the Differences

Everyone Leads
**It takes each of us to make
a difference for all of us**

Expect Success
Our Commitment to Our Customer

Forever Remembered
A Gift for the Grieving Heart

I Believe in You
**To your heart, your dream, and the
difference you make**

Little Miracles
**Cherished messages of hope,
joy, love, kindness and courage**

Reach for the Stars
Give up the good to go for the great

Team Works
Working Together Works

Thank You
**In appreciation of you, and
all that you do**

To Your Success
**Thoughts to Give Wings to
Your Work and Your Dreams**

Together We Can
**Celebrating the power of a
team and a dream**

What's Next
Creating the Future Now

Whatever It Takes
**A Journey into the Heart
of Human Achievement**

You've Got a Friend
**Thoughts to Celebrate the
Joy of Friendship**